Understanding Boat Corrosion, Lightning Protection and Interference

Understanding Boat Corrosion, Lightning Protection and Interference

JOHN C. PAYNE

SHERIDAN HOUSE

This edition first published 2005 by
Sheridan House Inc.
145 Palisade Street,
Dobbs Ferry, NY 10522

Library of Congress Cataloging-In-Publication Data

Payne, John C.
    Understanding boat corrosion, lightning protection, and
interference / John C. Payne.
        p. cm.
    ISBN 1-57409-199-9 (alk. paper)
        1. Boats and boating—Corrosion. 2. Ships—Cathodic protection.
    3. Seawater corrosion. 4. Boats and boating—Safety measures.
    5. Lightning protection. 6. Radio on boats. 7. Radio—
    Interference—Prevention. I. Title.
    VM951.P39 2004
    623.8'48—dc22   2004020344

Printed in the United States of America
ISBN 1-57409-199-9

Contents

1.

GALVANIC CORROSION

Some corrosion history

If there is to be galvanic corrosion, there has to be a potential difference between each of the metals. This principle was discovered in the eighteenth century by Luigi Galvani (where the word galvanic comes from). It involved experiments with the nerves and muscles of a frog; they contracted when hooked up to a bimetallic conductor. This developed into the first practical battery cell by Alessandro Volta (where the word volt comes from).

What is corrosion?

Corrosion can be defined as the chemical deterioration, or reduction, of a metal or metal alloy due to interaction with the environment. In the corrosion process, metal atoms leave the metal to form compounds in the presence of water or gases. This is commonly called rusting. Corrosion is often improperly called electrolysis. Corrosion takes many forms. For boats and basic electrical systems corrosion falls into two main categories: galvanic corrosion and electrolytic or stray current corrosion. Stray current corrosion is damage resulting from current flow outside the intended circuit.

What is galvanic corrosion?

Galvanic corrosion or electro-chemical corrosion is the process that occurs when galvanic cells or couples form between two pieces of metal with different electrochemical potential when they come into contact with each other. If the two metals have the same electrical charge or potential they will not create a cell, so no current will flow, and they are called compatible. Four basic conditions must be present for corrosion to occur.

1. There has to be a positive or anodic area. It is called the anode and possesses the lowest potential. It is the metal that will corrode.

2. There has to be a negative or cathodic area. It is called the cathode and possesses the highest potential.

3. There has to be a path for the current to flow. This is called the electrolyte. This is the water.

4. There has to be a circuit path for the current to flow. This is any interconnecting material.

Figure 1-1 Galvanic Corrosion Process

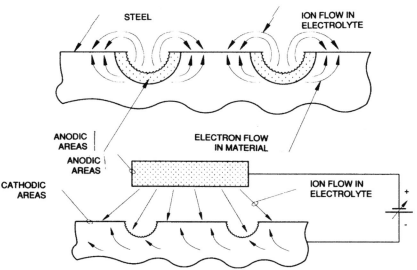

How does galvanic corrosion work?

When two different metals with a different potential are connected via an external wire connection, or are in contact and placed in a current-conducting electrolyte such as seawater, a galvanic cell is created at the interface between the metal and the electrolyte. This will cause the base metal to corrode. The corrosion reaction takes place on the two dissimilar metals that are electrically connected. The result is pitting and corrosion of propellers, split pins, stern tubes, shafts, shaft p-brackets, rudders and hangings, rudderstocks and any other incompatible underwater metallic items.

Figure 1-2 Vessel Galvanic Corrosion

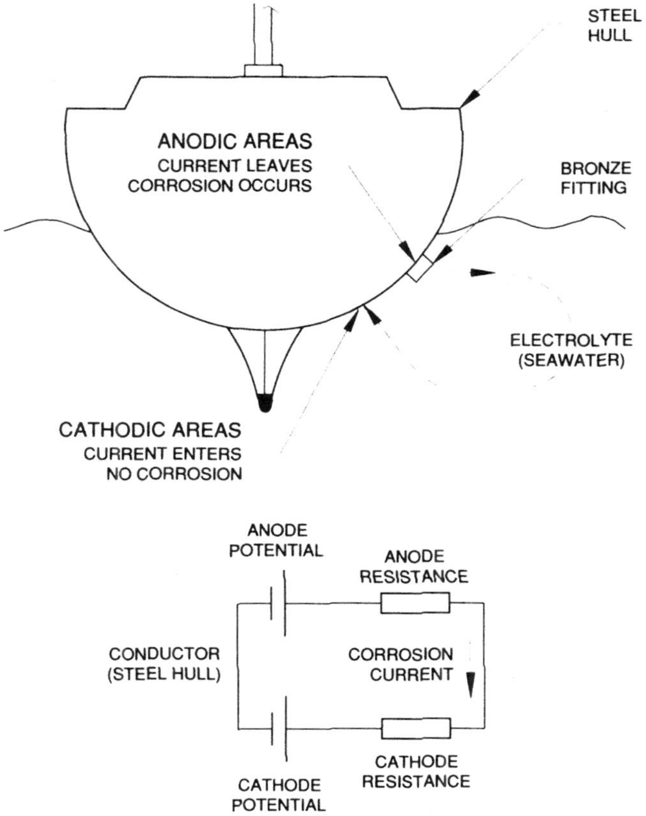

What factors affect the corrosion process?

The rate of corrosion is affected by several factors. These include the anodic corrosion current level, the water temperature and the water salinity. A basic parameter is derived from Faraday's Law, which is that a known current acting for a known time will cause a predictable weight loss of metal. For example, 1 amp applied for 1 year will cause a loss of 22lbs (10kg) of steel. The size of the exposed area of the cathodic metal relative to the anodic metal also will affect the corrosion rate. The corrosion rate varies between metals. The corrosion current within systems is typically rated within thousandths of an ampere, or milliamperes (mA).

What is the metal nobility scale?

All metals can be classified according to molecular structure. These characteristics are listed in a metal nobility table. The base metals at the top of the scale conduct easily, while the noble metals at the bottom do not. The materials with the greatest negative value will tend to corrode faster than those of a lesser potential. All metals can corrode, both ferrous and non-ferrous. Base metals such as steel and aluminum corrode more easily than the noble metals such as stainless steel and bronze. The voltage difference between metals will drive current flow to accelerate corrosion of the anodic metal.

Metal Galvanic Series Nobility Table

Metal	Voltage
Magnesium and alloys	− 1.65 V
Zinc plating on steel	− 1.30 V
Zinc	− 1.10 V
Galvanized iron	− 1.05 V
Aluminum alloy castings	− 0.75 V
Mild steel	− 0.70 V
Cast iron	− 0.70 V
Lead	− 0.55 V
Manganese bronze	− 0.27 V
Copper, brass and bronze	− 0.25 V
Monel	− 0.20 V
Stainless steel (passive)	− 0.20 V
Nickel (passive)	− 0.15 V
Silver	− 0.00 V
Gold	+ 0.15 V

What is galvanic protection?

The British Admiralty introduced anodic protection back in 1824 on copper-clad timber men-of-war sailing ships. A vessel should be constructed so that most metallic items are compatible. If they are, there are no potential differences, so no current will flow, and there will be no corrosion. If the materials in contact are different, they must be isolated with physical barriers between the dissimilar metals, or be protected.

Figure 1-3 Galvanic Protection

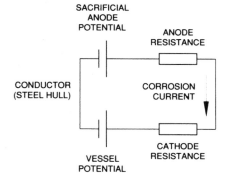

How does corrosion protection work?

Since four conditions are required for corrosion to occur, the elimination of one or more will prevent or mitigate the corrosion process. This generally entails the elimination of all the anodic areas on the boat. The most common method of protection is the use of a sacrificial metal or anode such as zinc, which has a higher natural electrical potential. It is connected by a conductor or wire to each item to be protected. This method uses the natural difference in electrical potential between the two metals to cause a protection current to flow. The driving voltage is very small due to the relatively low electrical potential that exists between the two metals and therefore the current is also relatively small.

What does a zinc anode do?

The zinc anode is still the most common protection method. Zinc anodes are used on most commercial vessels, offshore and pleasure boats. They are used in everything from internal supertanker ballast tanks, ships hulls, to the internal spaces of submarine sonar arrays. Some equipment manufacturers call them "old fashioned"; however they are still used because of their effectiveness. The average vessel uses zinc sacrificial anodes for corrosion protection.

Why are zincs called sacrificial?

They are called sacrificial because they are sacrificed instead of the item they are attached to, such as the hull, shaft, and rudder or trim tabs. As zincs are high on the nobility scale, and have a higher electrical potential, they will corrode a lot faster than other metals, such as mild steel. Pure zinc anodes are good conductors and generate an electric current. Since the hull or protected item effectively has a higher potential than the anode, this allows current flow through it and bonded items to the seawater, and back to the hull. The process corrodes the anode in proportion to the level of current flow present, while preserving the base metal, such as the hull or fittings.

About zinc use in fresh water

Houseboats, canal boats, barges and other vessels on freshwater lakes, rivers and canals follow the same criteria as boats in salt water. The major difference is that anodes are made from either magnesium or aluminum. Fresh water has a much greater insulation value than salt water, so anodes such as magnesium and aluminum with a higher driving voltage than zinc anodes, are required. When a boat moves into seawater or water of a higher salinity, anodes will become more active and should be inspected after just 14 days.

Where should zinc anodes be installed?

Anode positioning is not critical but they must be able to "see" or be visible to the parts that are to be protected. This means that installing zincs remotely, even if bonded, does not really protect fittings. In a sailing yacht they are installed midway between the propeller and the engine.

What about zinc purity standards?

Quality zincs are essential for good cathodic protection. You must beware of the quality of cheap imports. Zinc alloy anodes should conform to US Mil Spec MIL-18001J or equivalent. If they do not have a standard quoted, exercise caution using them.

Do I have to connect everything?

In reality, most modern fiberglass (GRP) vessels don't need very much protection. The general rule of bonding all electrically isolated metal thru-hull fittings interconnected in a daisy-chain arrangement, to keep them at the same potential, is flawed. It probably causes far more harm than good. This may be at variance with some recommendations. If all the underwater items are of the same material, that is bronze, and are electrically isolated by hoses that are rubber or PVC, there is no reason to protect them. If there are no dissimilar metals there can be no corrosion cell formation. If you bond everything and then connect into other systems, you create a situation where outside influences, such as stray current, can cause problems. Remember: you protect only those items that are close to other items underwater of dissimilar metal. This is usually in the stern, and covers propeller shafts, brackets, rudder hangings, etc.

Bonding and grounding systems explained

When boaters are asked what their bonding system does, or why it is installed, very few are able to provide a technically valid answer. In most cases indiscriminate bonding is performed without any defined purpose. It is important at this stage to explain and define clearly what the various "grounds" on a boat are. It is very important to understand these definitions as there is often much confusion, which is a key contributor to corrosion problems.

1. **Cathodic Protection System Ground.** The cathodic protection system equipotential bonding, or system ground, connects the sacrificial anode to the underwater items to be protected. This is to maintain all items at equal electrical potential. It is not to assist in dissipating stray currents.

2. **DC Negative Ground.** The DC negative in a single circuit wiring configuration is bonded to a grounded point, usually the mass of the engine. The engine is connected to an immersed item such as the steel hull or prop shaft. This is used to polarize the electrical system and doesn't actually carry current.

3. **Lightning Ground.** A lightning ground is a point at ground potential that is immersed in seawater. It only carries current in the event of a lightning strike. Its primary purpose is to effectively carry to ground that strike energy. It is not a functional part of any other electrical system.

4. **AC Ground (or Earth).** The AC safety ground is a point at ground potential. Under normal operating conditions, it carries no voltage or current. The primary purpose is that, under fault conditions, it will safely carry fault current to ground and hold all connected metal to ground potential, and ensure operation of protective equipment such as fuses and circuit breakers. This is to protect people against electric shock from exposed metal parts. Disconnection of an AC ground can cause serious electric shock or electrocution. Never disconnect the AC ground in your shorepower plug or socket to reduce possible corrosion. Several people have been electrocuted due to this irresponsible action. As a note of caution, most AC grounds are connected on board at the same point as the DC system polarizing ground. ABYC and other organizations recommend this and the reason is that should a short circuit or leakage condition develop between AC and DC, this will ensure that the AC system protection devices will still operate. If this did not happen the DC system and any connected equipment could be alive up to rated voltage, creating a risk to those in the water and on board. This bonding recommendation has created much controversy and the corrosion aspect is the main point. Always make sure that installed AC and DC systems are completely apart to prevent this relatively uncommon scenario. Also make sure that AC safety ground is regularly serviced and in good condition.

5. **Radio Frequency Ground.** The radio frequency ground is an integral part of the aerial system and is sometimes termed the counterpoise. The ground only carries RF energy and is not a current carrying conductor. It is not normally connected to any other ground or negative.

6. **Instrument Ground.** The instrument ground, which most GPS and radar sets have, is the nominal vessel ground. In many cases, a complete separate ground terminal link is installed behind the switchboard, to which the screens and ground wires are connected. A separate large low-resistance cable is then taken to the same ground point as other grounds. Do not simply interconnect the DC negative to the link as equipment may be subject to interference.

What type of wire should be used?

All bonding cables or wires must be of at least a 4.0-mm^2 tinned-copper conductor. This ensures low resistance and also some protection against corrosion. Every resistance within a circuit affects the functional ability of the system. This means that the proper cable size and resistance along with terminations all have an impact on performance. Do not use a stainless or exposed bare wire as is often done.

How should the bonding conductor be installed?

All cathodic protection system bonding cables should be run clear of bilges or other wet locations. They should only interconnect the items to be protected, and should not indiscriminately bond all items.

About keeping resistance low

The total resistance of any cathodic bonding circuit should not exceed 0.02 ohm. The purpose of bonding is to equalize the electric potential of the underwater metals being connected. It is not to dissipate stray currents on a 12-volt system and spread the surface areas. It is critical that bonding cables be resistance free and, therefore, use of a heavy gauge conductor is necessary. When the vessel is hauled, use a multimeter set on the 1-ohm range and check the resistance between anode and propeller. The maximum reading must be 0.02 ohm. The current flow in a bonding circuit is very small and any resistance introduced into the circuit from bad connections and cable resistances creates a difference in potential. It will cancel any protective measures and may actually create problems.

About bonding thru-hull fittings

No grounding connections should be made to any hull fitting or plumbing system unless absolutely necessary. Do not indiscriminately bond hull fittings and seacocks to the system. Only parts being protected should be bonded. This is at variance to ABYC; however, I have come across far too many problems directly attributable to this.

About bonding lightning systems

The bonding system should not be connected to the lightning protection system. Do not bond the lightning ground system or the down conductor to the anode bonding system. This is at variance to ABYC. However, there have been several well-documented cases of hull fittings being blown out in a lightning strike and the vessel subsequently sinking. Read the section on lightning bonding.

Can I bond different metals?

Ferrous and non-ferrous metals should not be bonded to the same anode. If you bond them it will effectively create a cell or battery.

What about aluminum boats?

There are many aluminum boats, both small and large. The systems and criteria are similar to the requirements for steel vessels. It is essential that hulls be correctly protected. Insulate or use compatible thru-hull fittings. Insulate any equipment made of differing metals above aluminum on the nobility scale. Many boats use plastic (Marelon) thru-hull valves and fittings, which solves many problems. Lloyd's and others approve all these. Do not use bronze fittings if at all possible. Avoid mooring next to steel or copper-sheathed vessels for extended periods. The interaction problem can be very severe with aluminum. Unlike steel vessels, an over-protected aluminum hull doesn't simply lose paint but it gets eaten away by a caustic attack. The recommendations for steel hulls are also valid. An insulated two wire electrical system is also recommended.

About stern gear bonding

The usual method for both commercial and small vessels is the installation of a brush system on the propeller. One such device is called the Electro Eliminator. Essentially, it is a simple brush system connected to the cathodic bonding system, or on steel boats grounded directly to the hull or central bonding point. The systems use copper graphite brushes, and quoted life is around 2000 hours. If such a system is used, the shaft must be kept clean and free of oil, grease and water. Slip rings are not the ideal solution for short length shafts. It is better to bridge the coupling to the engine block and use a collar anode or separate anode bonded directly to the engine block. Many engine installations incorporate flexible couplings on the propeller shaft. The coupling must be electrically bridged to ensure proper continuity of the shaft system where the engine is not maintained electrically isolated above the bonding system.

Figure 1-4 Propeller Shaft Bonding

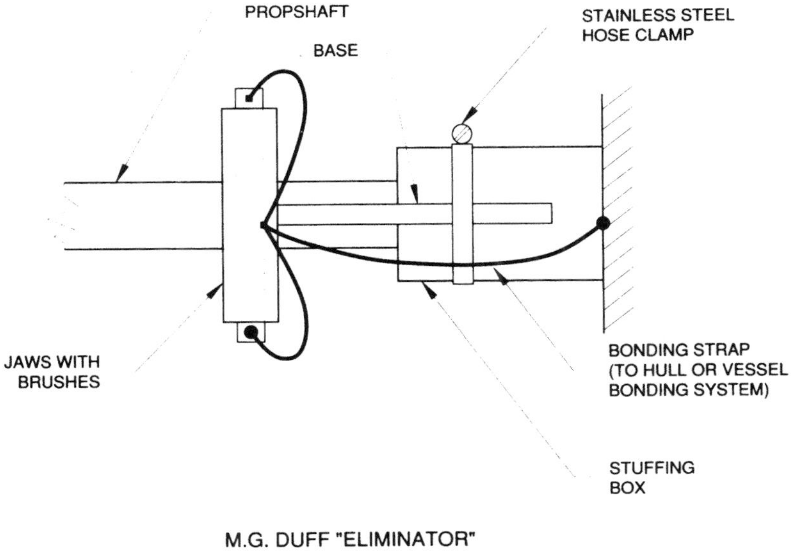

PROPSHAFT

BASE

STAINLESS STEEL
HOSE CLAMP

JAWS WITH
BRUSHES

BONDING STRAP
(TO HULL OR VESSEL
BONDING SYSTEM)

STUFFING
BOX

M.G. DUFF "ELIMINATOR"

About anode sizes

These are based on recommendations by leading corrosion specialists for fiberglass (GRP) and wooden vessels. Consult them for specific boat applications. The anode sizes are based on propeller sizes and are approximate only.

Type A Vessels

Type A vessels are generally single-screw boats with a short propeller shaft length in contact with seawater. They have wooden or fiberglass (GRP) rudders. Normally only one anode is required for propeller and shaft protection. The main anode should be located on the hull below the turn of bilge, at an equal distance between the gearbox and the inboard end of the stern tube.

Figure 1-5 Anode Arrangements

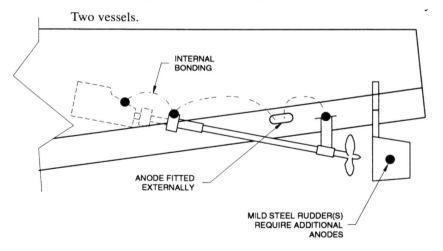

Type B Vessels.

Type B vessels are single- or twin-screw boats with long exposed propeller shafts supported by a shaft bracket and in contact with seawater. One anode is required for each propeller and shaft assembly. Separate anodes are required for mild steel rudders. Bronze or stainless steel rudders with bronze or stainless steel rudderstocks must be bonded to the same anode.

Type C Vessels.

Type C vessels are single-screw boats with long exposed propeller shafts supported by a shaft bracket and in contact with seawater. They have fiberglass (GRP) rudders and bronze or stainless steel rudderstocks. Normally only one anode is required for propeller and shaft protection. Mild steel bilge keels should have separate anodes affixed.

Type D Vessels.

Type D vessels are stern-drive boats fitted with outdrive units. Outdrive units normally have manufacturer-designed and supplied anodes. Where no anodes are installed, a small round anode may be installed on the hull and bonded to the leg.

Can I put on too many zincs?

You should install only the zincs required to do the job. If several extra zincs are installed to give better protection the opposite effect will occur. One sign of excess zinc installation is a layer of zinc oxide over items to be protected, such as the propeller.

How many zincs are needed?

This depends entirely on the situation. In most sailing boats, one
zinc plus a shaft anode will usually suffice. With steel boats, this
is based on a wetted surface-area calculation.

To select the size of anode required for fiberglass (GRP) and
wooden boats, determine the type of vessel, A, B or C, and the
size of the propeller installed.

Anode Mass Table (Salt and Fresh Water)

Prop Size	Type A	Type B	Type C
10" SW zinc	1.1 kg	2 x 1 kg	1.1 kg
FW magnesium	0.3 kg	2 x 0.3 kg	0.3 kg
14" SW zinc	1.1 kg	2 x 1 kg	1.1 kg
FW magnesium	0.3 kg	2 x 0.3 kg	0.3 kg
19" SW zinc	2.2 kg	2 x 1 kg	2.2 kg
FW magnesium	0.4 kg	2 x 0.4 kg	0.4 kg
21" SW zinc	2.2 kg	2 x 2.2 kg	2.2 kg
FW magnesium	0.7 kg	2 x 0.7 kg	0.7 kg
26" SW zinc	2.2 kg	2 x 2.2 kg	2.2 kg
FW magnesium	0.7 kg	2 x 1.0 kg	0.7 kg
30" SW zinc	2.2 kg	2 x 2.2 kg	2.2 kg
FW magnesium	0.7 kg	1 kg	1 kg
36" SW zinc	4.5 kg	2 x 4.5 kg	4.5 kg
FW magnesium	1 kg	1 kg	1 kg
40" SW zinc	4.5 kg	2 x 4.5 kg	4.5 kg
FW magnesium	1 kg	2 x 1 kg	1 kg
48" SW zinc	4.5 kg	2 x 4.5 kg	4.5 kg

Note: 1kg = 2.2 lbs

About fiberglass (GRP) and wooden boat anodes

1. **Location.** The anode fixing studs must be above the bilge line internally, and there must be a minimal internal bonding cable length. They must not be installed forward of the speed log and depth transducers as the flow will cause problems. Make sure you can access the bolts internally.

2. **Anode Backing Sheets.** An anode backing sheet must be installed behind each anode when installed against the hull. The sheet helps control the anode wastage.

3. **Seal Anode Bolt Holes.** Always seal the wood both in and around the anode bolt holes with silicon sealant. This will reduce wood decay and corrosion.

4. **Connection.** Fan disc washers are used under the anode securing nuts to ensure a good low resistance contact. When the anode is replaced, they will also need to be replaced.

Steel boat protection explained

Corrosion risks are significantly greater on steel vessels. The following precautions must be observed to reduce galvanic and electrolytic corrosion. Good protection on steel is also very much a function of a properly planned and applied painting program. Use the technical services of your paint supplier in addition to the protection measures described.

Anode Number Calculations. Calculations are normally based on wetted surface-area calculations. The main vessel dimensions used are waterline length, breadth and mean loaded draft. Area is calculated using the formula:

Length Water Line (LWL) x (Breadth + Draft)

This formula will suit most motor-cruisers, trawler yachts, canal boats and barges. For medium density vessels, multiply the calculated sum by 0.75. For light displacement vessels multiply by 0.5. Based on this calculation, look at the anode selection table. Two-year protection offers approximately 50% greater anode quantities. Anodes either are welded on, or are bolt-on stud mounted.

One-Year Anode Selection Table

Wetted Area	Hull Anodes	Rudders
Up to 28 m^2 (300ft^2) SW	2 x 4.0 kg zinc	2 x 1.0 kg zinc
Up to 28 m^2 (300ft^2) FW	4 x 1.5 kg mag	2 x 0.3 kg mag
28.1 - 56 m^2 (>600ft^2) SW	4 x 3.5 kg zinc	2 x 1.0 kg zinc
28.1 - 56 m^2 (>600ft^2) FW	4 x 3.5 kg mag	2 x 0.3 kg mag
56.1 - 84 m^2 (>900ft^2) SW	4 x 4.0 kg zinc	2 x 1.0 kg zinc
56.1 - 84 m^2 (>900ft^2) FW	4 x 3.5 kg mag	2 x 0.3 kg mag
84.1 - 102 m^2 (>1100ft^2) SW	4 x 6.5 kg zinc	2 x 2.2 kg zinc
84.1 - 102 m^2 (>1100ft^2) FW	6 x 4.5 kg mag	2 x 0.7 kg mag
102.1 - 148 m^2 (>1600ft^2) t) SW	6 x 6.5 kg zinc	2 x 2.2 kg zinc

Note: 1kg = 2.2 lbs

Shaft collar anodes

When fitting collar anodes make sure that the shaft is clean, and not placed over an antifouled shaft. The anode must make good electrical contact. The collars must be mounted as close as possible to the shaft support bracket, typically a clearance of 4–10 mm. Do not antifoul the anode! It is surprising how often this happens. In many cases the anode fastening bolts are not to the correct torque; it comes loose and disappears very quickly.

Figure 1-6 Shaft Anode Installation

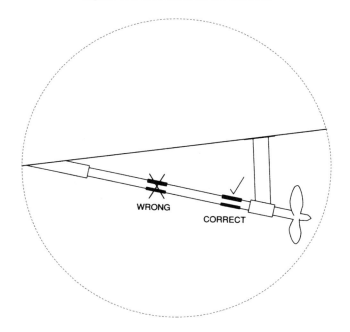

Signs of stern-drive corrosion problems

The first indicators of impending corrosion are signs of paint blistering. This can mostly be observed on sharp edges. Exposed aluminum surfaces such as those on paint chips, etc., start to form powdery white deposits. This leads eventually to pitting.

Why aren't the anodes corroding?

If a stern-drive unit shows some corrosion and there is no corrosion activity on the anodes, this indicates a problem that must be addressed. This is usually caused by poor electrical contacts between the anode and the stern-drive unit. They should be removed, the mounting surfaces cleaned, and anodes reinstalled.

About electrical continuity

The entire bonding system must be electrically near perfect with low resistance if it is to function correctly. In stern-drive units and outboards, stainless steel braided conductors are used between the drive shaft housings and brackets. Wave washers are also used to maintain good electrical contact. If the interconnections are poor, corrosion will start.

About stern-drive protection systems

Some drives such as Volvo and Mercury (MerCathode) have an active electronic anti-corrosion system. They use a reference anode and an active anode. The reference senses surrounding seawater potential, and the control unit sends a current to the active anode. These anodes emit varying levels of ions into the water surrounding the drive. They complement the zinc anodes, but they do not replace them. This is an impressed current type system.

What are electrical antifouling systems?

These units should not be confused with cathodic protection systems. Units such as those from Cathelco and Jotun are used for protecting sea chests and seawater inlets against fouling by marine growth. They use a copper anode, which releases copper ions into the system, and acts as an antifoulant. They are used on larger vessels only.

What corrosion system maintenance is required?

1. **Main Anodes.** Do an underwater check of anodes after six months for increased corrosion rates. If the vessel has moved into warmer or more saline conditions, rates increase. Rapid zinc loss and shiny zincs indicate a stray current problem.

2. **Shaft Anodes.** Check that the shaft anode is still on the shaft. Check the anode corrosion rates.

What haul-out inspections are required?

1. **Anode Replacement.** Replace anodes if they are more than 75% reduced, and check connections.

2. **Shaft Anodes.** Replace anode if necessary. Check mating surface of shaft anode. Check that it is correctly located.

3. **Bonding Connections.** Inspect bonding system interconnections to see that they are sound and clean. Remove connections and clean them, so that contact resistance is virtually nil.

4. **Check Bonding System Resistances.** Check bonding resistances between the anodes, and propeller and hull.

Troubleshooting zinc anodes

White or green halos around zincs or metals indicate that stray current is affecting them. Bright zincs indicate excess current flow, usually from a stray current condition. A small amount of current also causes paint reactions. Rapid zinc wastage and degree of paint reaction indicate problems that are more serious. If a boat has moved into fresh water and back to salt, the anode will become encrusted with a white crust. This will stop it functioning and it must be cleaned off. In general, some oxide crust will build up and require removal as it tends to inhibit corrosion rates.

Using corrosion monitors

The voltage on the hull relative to seawater can be monitored using a reference cell. The meter indicates when a problem exists, often using red, yellow and green markings.

What about portable corrosion testers?

Verifying the condition of a corrosion protection system requires the testing and the measurement of the hull potential. This involves the immersion of a reference electrode called a half-cell. This half-cell is made from silver/silver chloride, which is a silver wire coated with silver chloride. The reference cell is immersed approximately 6 inches into the water around the hull. The reference electrode is connected to a digital multimeter positive terminal. The negative terminal is connected to the boat ground, which is usually the battery negative ground point. The multimeter is then set to the 2-volt DC scale or simple DC volts on most as they are auto-ranging. This will display a value, which is the actual hull potential. The readings must be interpreted according to water temperature and salinity.

Corrosion system troubleshooting

The anodes are corroding rapidly

1. Hull electrical leakages. Check your electrical system.

2. Increased water salinity.

3. Increased water temperature.

4. Degraded bonding system. Check that all connections are clean and secure.

5. Moored adjacent to a vessel made from alloy or steel.

6. Marina electrical problems. Usually the last on the list.

The propeller and shaft are pitted

1. Impure zinc anode. Check the standard of zinc installed.

2. Inadequate protection. Insufficient zincs installed or one is missing.

3. Degraded bonding system. Check that all connections are clean and secure.

4. Shaft anode missing. Check that it is still there.

5. Shaft anode fitted over antifouled shaft.

6. Cavitation corrosion.

There is no anode corrosion

1. Anode stud connection defective.

2. Anode hull connections defective.

3. Bonding wires broken.

What is impressed current cathodic protection?

These systems are installed on larger steel and alloy vessels. Protection is based on the compensation of corrosion currents by a counter current using an on-board power source. The reference anode senses the electrical potential of the seawater and sends a signal to the control unit, which then puts out an appropriate current to the active anode. The protective current is transmitted through the electrolyte to the areas under protection. The area under protection is converted into a cathode, preventing metal corrosion. Zinc anodes have very low and non-variable driving voltages with reduced effectiveness. The varying combinations of water temperature, chemical composition and exposed surface require monitoring, and may require different current levels. The anode is made of a relatively inert material such as silicon iron, silver/lead alloys, tantalum or platinum. The driving voltage and current outputs are adjusted at the power source to enable precise control. Corrosion will be inhibited as long as the protective potential is applied. In normal operation, mechanically damaged or porous hull areas will have an insulation layer form over them, caused by salts and the current flow.

Figure 1-7 Impressed Current Protection Systems

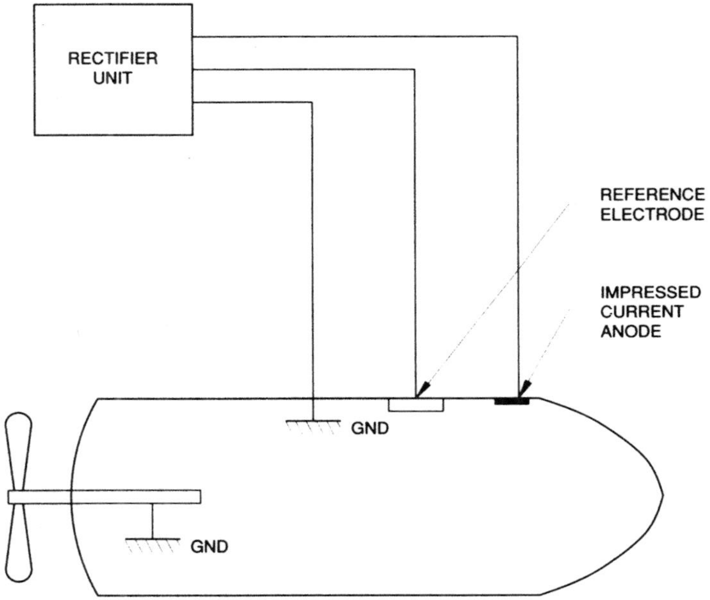

2.

STRAY
CURRENT
CORROSION

What is electrolytic (stray current) corrosion?

This is often improperly called electrolysis. A number of factors must be considered. Electrolytic corrosion has different principles from galvanic corrosion, and they should not be confused. Protective measures for galvanic corrosion do not protect against electrolytic corrosion. Stray current corrosion will dramatically increase corrosion rates on underprotected hulls and anodes, degrading the galvanic protective system. If faults are left undiagnosed, anodes will rapidly degrade, followed by loss of paint and antifouling. A complete repainting of the hull, from metal primer upwards, may be required.

About internal stray current corrosion

A DC source starts from within a boat electrical system and leaks to ground through a bonding system that is connected to various underwater items, and that creates corrosion. The sources are usually damp electrical equipment connections such as bilge and shower pumps. Another common source of leakage is across battery top surfaces or within engine equipment such as the starter motor and solenoid positive terminals.

About external stray current corrosion

A DC current is carried aboard a boat through a shorepower AC safety ground connection. All boats in a marina that are connected to shore power are effectively bonded together. This creates a circuit between boats and DC current will flow. When the boat AC safety ground is bonded to a cathodic protection or general bonding system, this current will be applied and cause corrosion to underwater items.

Can AC cause corrosion?

Generally, AC does not cause corrosion. AC must be rectified to DC to cause corrosion. I have had questions regarding rectification through various fittings on a boat. Although relatively rare, it is possible for some materials to form a device similar to semiconductor diode causing some partial half-wave rectification. Most blame is attributed to faulty AC system wiring but in reality I have encountered very few boats with AC ground faults. There is no such thing on a boat, although it is known to exist in large underground pipelines.

What is a galvanic isolator?

These devices are designed to provide galvanic isolation of the AC shore ground from a DC bonding system when they are connected. In boats without inverters or generators, the main ground is effectively the shore ground, as no on board grounding is usually installed. In effect, the vessel is simply an appliance at the end of an extension cable, much like a trailer. In this mode, any DC currents imposed on the AC system will not affect the boat. When the boat has an AC system that is bonded to the DC and cathodic or bonding systems, this provides a path for DC stray leakage currents to the DC power system, to the immersed parts of the boat such as the propeller, and the cathodic protection system.

How is a galvanic isolator constructed?

A galvanic isolator has an electrical circuit that incorporates diodes, configured to block DC current flow. It also incorporates capacitors, which allow the AC to bypass the diodes. The AC flows from the boat to shore in a fault condition and must be able to pass very low AC leakage currents.

Choosing the right isolator

You must install the correctly rated isolator. A 50-amp supply requires a 50-amp rated isolator, and a 30-amp supply requires a 30-amp rated isolator. When a boat has two shorepower inlets each must have a separate isolator installed. If an underrated isolator is used, it will burn out under full fault conditions.

Installing galvanic isolators

Isolators must be installed close to the shorepower inlet socket. They also must be installed in a well-ventilated location as they can become very hot in a fault current conducting mode. The American Boat and Yacht Council (ABYC) recommends that no part of the AC grounding system should bypass the galvanic isolator. This would allow leakage currents to come aboard.

Monitoring an isolator

If an isolator is installed within the AC safety ground, monitoring the integrity is of critical importance. Testing will ensure that it can safely conduct AC fault currents at all times and that the device has not failed. One method often quoted is to touch with the hand to see if it is warm. By this time, it is far too late and a dangerous condition already exists on board. In accordance with ABYC recommendations many isolators have a monitor with an LED indicator that displays functioning of diodes and capacitors, along with AC safety ground continuity, reverse polarity and more.

Why are isolation transformers used?

For many steel and alloy vessels, the first method of isolating the electrical system is to use an isolation transformer. This is a one-to-one ratio transformer that galvanically, or as some say, magnetically isolates the boat's electrical system from the shore. One great myth is that transformers are inefficient with large power losses. In fact a transformer is the most efficient of all electrical equipment at around 98%. It is simple, uncomplicated and reliable; the only drawback is weight.

Figure 2-1 220/240 VAC ShorePower Isolation Systems

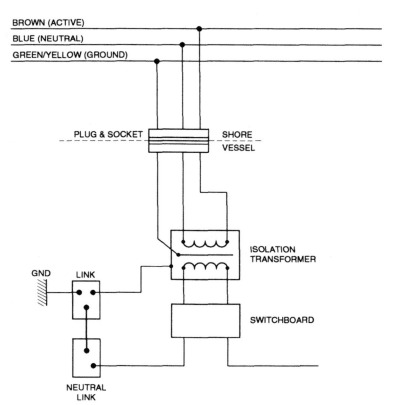

What is a leakage current?

Leakage currents are not nearly as common as portrayed in many magazine articles. They are mostly caused by electrical leakages across condensation or conductive salt deposits at DC connections or junction boxes, or tracking from main starter motor cables. 24- and 48-volt systems have higher risks than 12-volt systems given the higher potential differences. In some cases, they may also be caused by damaged insulation. A properly installed electrical system offers few opportunities for the situation to arise. The most common area is tracking across engine starter motor and solenoid connections, which may not be sufficiently clean of grease, oil or moisture.

What is a ground fault?

Ground faults on AC and DC conductors occur when the cable insulation has been damaged and contact is made with the hull or connected metalwork. In many cases, the fault may not be sufficient to operate protective devices and remain unnoticed for a considerable and damaging period. The most common areas causing faults are where cables enter grounded stainless steel stanchions, alloy masts, engine charging and starter cables. In any area where a cable can contact grounded metal, leakage or fault currents can happen. Install a leakage test lamp unit that handles both AC and DC, so that the hull can be monitored continuously, and any problems found and rectified promptly. This is the standard commercial ship practice, checked daily with all leakages and faults corrected promptly.

What about steel/alloy hull leakage inspections?

It is always difficult to maintain a steel or alloy hull above ground. Moisture and oil residues mixed with salt lower the isolation level. It is important to regularly examine isolation values to ensure that it is maintained. These tests assume that all electrical systems, instrumentation, etc., are insulated two-wire above hull systems. The galvanic bonding system is also an independent system.

What is a passive insulation test?

This test measures the level of resistance between the hull and the positive and negative circuits. A multimeter set on the ohm scale is required. Perform the test as follows:

1. Turn main power switch off.

2. Turn on all switches and circuit breakers to ensure that all electrical circuits are at equal potential or connected in one grid.

3. Connect the positive meter lead to the positive conductor, and the negative to the hull. Observe and record the reading.

4. Connect the positive meter lead to the negative conductor, and the negative to the hull. Observe and record the reading.

Figure 2-2 Passive Testing

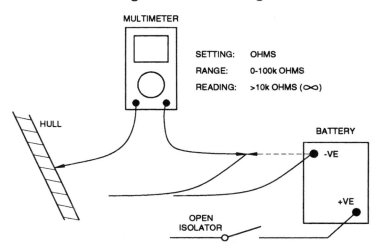

What do the passive test results mean?

The test results can be interpreted as follows:

1. 10k ohms or above indicates that isolation above hull is acceptable.

2. A reading in the range of 1k ohm to 10k ohms indicates that there is leakage, and the isolation is degraded. While not directly short circuited to the hull, leakage can occur through moisture or a similar cause. With a meter connected, systematically switch off each circuit to localize the fault area and rectify. A common area is the starter motor connections.

3. A reading less than 1k ohm indicates a serious leakage problem that must be promptly localized and rectified or serious hull damage can result.

What is a voltage insulation test?

Because a system in use is not passive, a voltage, and therefore a difference in potential exists. While a passive meter test can show all is satisfactory, a voltage can break down the resistances and cause leakage. To properly test the electrical isolation, a voltage test should be performed. With 220/115-volt mains systems this test must be performed using a 500-volt insulation tester and all results must exceed 1 meg ohm. This is not recommended for low voltage installations, as the insulation values of cables are not rated this high. A low-voltage DC tester should be used set at 100 volts DC.

How do you carry out the test?

Here is another easier test:

1. Turn on all electrical circuits so that all are "alive."

2. With a digital multimeter set on the DC volts place the positive probe on the supply negative. Place the negative probe on the hull.

3. There should be no voltage at all. If there is a small voltage, a leakage may exist on the negative.

4. With a digital multimeter set on the DC volts scale, place the negative probe on the supply negative. Place the positive probe on the hull.

5. There should be no voltage at all. If there is a small voltage, a leakage may exist on the positive.

6. Systematically turn off electrical circuits to verify that there is a leakage, and that, with all power off, the difference in potential is zero.

Figure 2-3 Insulation Testing

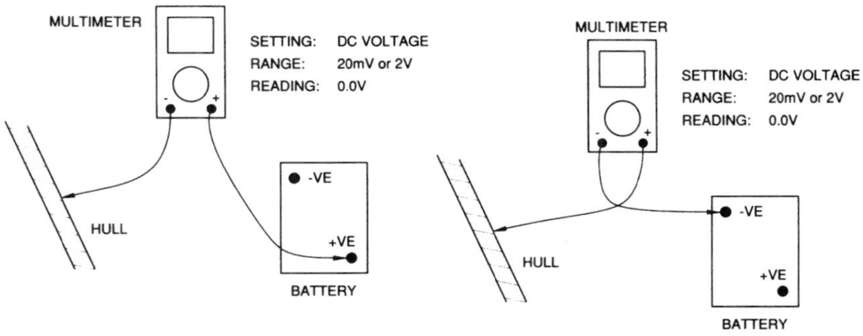

3.

LIGHTNING PROTECTION

What causes lightning?

Within the cloud formation, strong updrafts and downdrafts generate high electrical charges. When the voltage reaches a sufficiently high level, both cloud to cloud and ground discharges occur.

a. **Negative Cloud to Ground.** These strikes occur when the ground is at positive polarity and the cloud's negative region attempts to equalize with ground.

b. **Positive Cloud to Ground.** The positively charged cloud top equalizes with the negative ground.

c. **Positive Ground to Cloud.** The positive charged ground equalizes with the negative charge cloud.

d. **Negative Ground to Cloud.** The negatively charged ground equalizes with the positive charged cloud top.

Figure 3-1 Cumulo-Nimbus Storm System

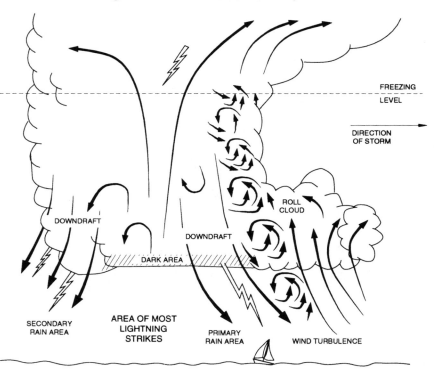

About lightning components

Lightning consists of a number of components that form a multidirectional flow of charges exceeding 200,000 amperes at over 30,000°C for a matter of milliseconds. The positively charged ions rise to the cloud top, and the negative ions migrate to the cloud base. Regions of positive charged ions also form at the cloud base. Eventually the cloud charge levels have sufficient potential difference between ground and another cloud to discharge.

Figure 3-2 Lightning Process

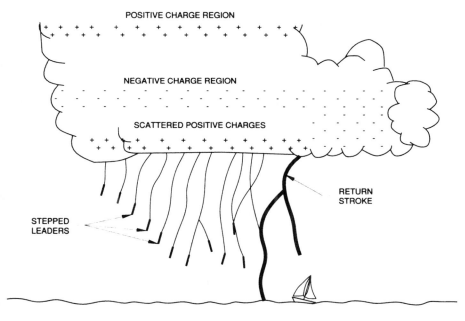

About the lightning strike process

Leader. The leader consists of a negative stream of electrons comprising many small forks or fingers that follow and break down the air paths offering the least resistance. The charge follows the fork, finding the easiest path as each successive layer is broken down and charged to the same polarity as the cloud charge.

Upward Positive Leader. This positive charge rises some 200 feet (50 meters) above the ground.

Channel. When leader and upward leader meet a channel is formed.

Return Stroke. This path is generally much brighter and more powerful than the leader. It travels upwards to the cloud, partially equalizing the potential difference between ground and cloud.

Dart Leader. In a matter of milliseconds after the return stroke, another downward charge takes place following the same path as the stepped leader and return stroke, sometimes followed by multiple return strokes. The movements happen so fast that it appears to be a single event. This sequence can continue until the differential between cloud and ground has been equalized.

About lightning safety and protection

All Class societies, Lloyd's, ABYC, NFPA, etc., make similar recommendations, but very few boats adhere to them. The empha-
sis has always been on sailing boats, but there are many instances
of power vessels also being hit with equally catastrophic results.
Many motorboats have prominent mast structures to carry radar,
navigation lights and large whip aerials; fly bridges have exten-
sive stainless steel tuna tower structures, trawler yachts and mo-
torsailers also have small masts, so protection should be
considered. More than a 1000 people are killed worldwide an-
nually by lightning strikes. In the US lightning transient damage
exceeds 1 billion dollars. Two great myths are: one, that a protection system is not designed to repel lightning; two, that having
a system attracts lightning.

What lightning standards are there?

1. ABYC Standard E-4, Lightning Protection, American Boat
   and Yacht Council
2. NFPA Standard 302, Chapter 9, Lightning Protection,
   National Fire Protection Association

Where are the worst lightning areas?

Lightning is one of nature's impressive sights. I am forever in awe
and can recall some spectacular shows. Places like the
Caribbean's Mona Passage spring to mind. Florida is probably
the lightning capital of the world. If you are sailing down to Key
West or along the Gulf Coast, your risks will be higher. Other locations such as Singapore, Northern Australia, the Western Pa-
cific Islands, and Central America are all considered high activity
areas.

What safety precautions do I take?

In an electrical storm, stay below decks at all times. Take a position and plot it prior to shutting down, or in case of all electronics equipment being blown. Turn off all electronic gear and isolate circuit breakers if at all possible. Disconnect aerials also if possible. Do not operate radios until after the storm, unless in an extreme emergency. Compasses should be rechecked and deviation corrections made after a strike. In some cases, complete demagnetization may occur.

How far away is the storm activity?

Thunder is caused by the heating of air to a very high temperature and the resultant shock wave during a strike. You can work out how far away the storm activity is by timing the flash to the arrival of the noise. The rule of thumb is to count one mile for every five seconds between flash and noise.

What is a lightning dissipation device?

A range of dissipation devices are available. These devices are typically brush or "bottle brush" type arrangements. The principle is that all the spikes bleed off or dissipate electrons or ions, reducing the differential that may cause a lightning strike. They do not protect the boat in the event of a strike, or safely carry strike energy to ground.

What is a lightning protection system?

Lightning has long been a problem for mariners. As far back as the early 1800s on old sailing ships, the boat builders were installing lightning protection systems to minimize the catastrophic effects of strikes. These methods were essentially based upon the grounding of spars and rigging. More than one vessel lost mizzens and masts along with subsequent electromagnetic pulse related compass problems as a result. Lightning protections systems also evolved as a response to dissipation of strike energy. There is some confusion as to what protection should be installed. This can never be achieved using a single method. A number of measures must be used to minimize the risks. The best security involves a holistic and overall systems approach. While not being completely adequate, given the raw natural power of lightning, the adoption of the following measures will at least minimize the effects:

1. The capture of the strike at a nominated point, i.e. the mast head.

2. The conduction of the strike current to ground safely using a well-installed down conductor that reduces side flashes.

3. The dissipation of the strike energy to ground, through a low impedance ground system so that rises in ground potential are minimized.

4. The equipotential ground bonding of all relevant systems and components.

5. The protection of power supplies from high voltage transients and surges that may damage equipment.

6. The protection of conductors both power and signal from induced surges that may damage equipment.

Lightning rods

A lightning conductor should be installed at the masthead. This should consist of a turned copper spike of at least 12mm in diameter, and projecting at least 150mm (6") above the highest point. The first element is the air terminal; ideally it should be a copper rod with pointed tip. The use of a rounded tip is also acceptable, given some more recent research. To avoid metal interaction, stainless rods are commonly used, but they should be of a thicker section than the more conductive and lower resistance copper. The spike should be at least six inches higher than any other equipment, including VHF aerials. This means a terminal 12–24" in height. Many commercial units have an offset in the rod, which although not the required straight section, would be satisfactory. The purpose of the sharp point is that it facilitates what is called point discharge. Ions dissipate from the ground and effectively cause a reduction in potential between the cloud and the sea. In many cases, the strike may be of lower intensity or not occur at all. Note that a stainless steel VHF whip aerial does not constitute any protection.

Figure 3-3 Masthead Protection Systems

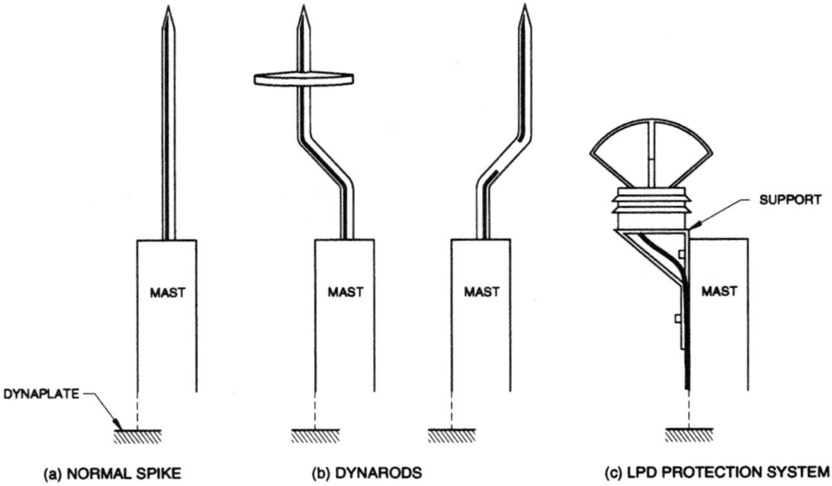

(a) NORMAL SPIKE   (b) DYNARODS   (c) LPD PROTECTION SYSTEM

What is the cone of protection?

The air terminal is mounted clear of all other equipment and gives a cone of protection below it. This protective cone prevents side strikes to adjacent areas and metalwork, which in a motorboat can mean rails or other items lower than the air terminal, or on a sailing boat, mast, spreaders, stays, shrouds and furling gear. Typically these may be on anything from navigation equipment on the stern, or on flybridges and tuna towers, stainless steel structures on fishing boats. The cone of protection is directly based on the height of the air terminal. A 50-foot mast with an air terminal will provide a 100-foot area of protection under it.

Figure 3-4 Cone of Protection

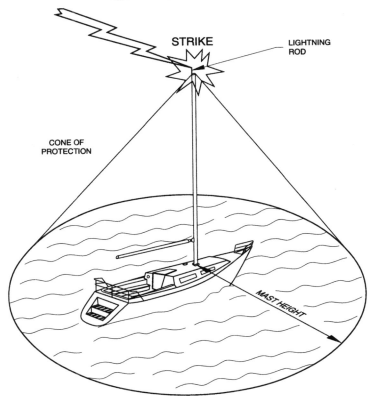

About circuit resistance

The total resistance of the grounding circuit from the lightning conductor to the ground plate or hull grounding point shall not exceed 0.02 ohm. A low resistance grounding circuit is absolutely critical to the performance of the protection system. Any resistance will cause significantly greater heating effects and strike energy will seek shorter and lower resistance ground paths. High resistance circuits will contribute to a higher probability of side strike activities. The NFPA has a specification that the resistance of the connection must not exceed that of a two-foot length of the down conductor.

Mast bonding explained

In vessels with alloy masts, the base of the mast should be bonded to the deck and mast step, or compression post. This should then be bonded to the ground plate or keel. It is often easier to bond the base of an alloy mast to the mast step, and then bond this to the compression post. The bottom of the compression post is then bonded to the ground plate or keel. Keel-stepped masts can be directly bonded to the ground plate or keel with a short and heavy gauge conductor. Wooden masts should have a conductor fastened externally to the mast. Some use a flat copper strip rather than a thick conductor, also bonding the external sail track.

About grounding chainplates and shrouds

There are some recommendations to bond the shrouds and chainplates to the lightning ground point. Besides spreading the strike energy a little further around the boat, this also creates an additional high impedance path down the stays and chainplates that can result in the crystallization of the stainless steel and possible loss of the rig under any tension. This should be avoided as it may fail while at sea. One major spar manufacturer voids all warranty on masts if they are struck by lightning because the heat can alter the metallurgical properties. It is imperative that a single, low resistance grounding system is installed.

About lightning down conductors

Lightning down conductors shall be of at least 100mm^2 (4 AWG) cross sectional area. Conductors should be run as straight as possible without sharp bends. The purpose of the down conductor is to safely conduct the strike current through a low impedance circuit, suitably rated, to carry the strike current to the ground point, and to eliminate side-flash dangers, to minimize induction into other conductors, and to maintain the strike period to the minimum possible. Much of the damage in a strike can result from heat, as the large current flow into even a low resistance down conductor cable can act as a large heating element. It is essential that the cable has a sufficient cross-sectional area, typically 4 AWG but preferably larger. The overall resistance of the cable must not exceed 0.02 ohm maximum. Electricity follows the path of least resistance, and this reduces side flash dangers if energy looks for alternative paths. This means that if a ground circuit is 2 ohms overall and a communications ground 1 ohm, the energy will divert through the communications ground. Welding cable is best as it has high voltage insulation in comparison to battery cables. In shore installations, special purpose triaxial cables are used. The multiple screens reduce the large radiated fields that are generated. However this is an expensive option, valid only on large super yachts. The bonding cable to the ground plate should be as straight as possible without sharp corners as side discharges, called corona discharge, will occur. It is also useful to enclose the conductor internally with PVC flexible conduit normally used in shore electrical systems to increase the insulation levels, as DC battery cable will break down under high voltage conditions.

What about ground plates?

The lightning conductor should be terminated at the hull, keel or an immersed ground plate with a minimum area of 0.2 m² (2 ft²). The ABYC calls for a minimum of 1 square foot made from copper, stainless steel or aluminum. In any boat the ground plane is seawater. Strike energy must be dissipated to ground with a minimal rise in ground potential through a low impedance earthing system. Steel and alloy boats use the hull as ground. In fiberglass (GRP) and wooden sailing boats, conductors are grounded on keel bolts. On most boats, you will have to install a large separate ground plate, such as a radio ground shoe, preferably the largest ones in the 50–100 square-foot range. This will ensure that there is a large and efficient ground area. Some quality shoes use a gold-based conductive grease under the bolt heads to ensure a good low resistance connection. Do not use the radio RF ground plate as the lightning ground.

Figure 3-5 Mast Grounding Arrangements

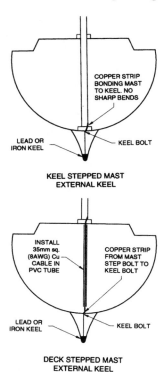

COPPER STRIP
BONDING MAST
TO KEEL. NO
SHARP BENDS

LEAD OR
IRON KEEL

KEEL BOLT

KEEL STEPPED MAST
EXTERNAL KEEL

INSTALL
35mm sq.
(8AWG) Cu
CABLE IN
PVC TUBE

COPPER STRIP
FROM MAST
STEP BOLT TO
KEEL BOLT

LEAD OR
IRON KEEL

KEEL BOLT

DECK STEPPED MAST
EXTERNAL KEEL

What about temporary grounds?

Many people use a plate on the end of a wire over the side and then clamp it to a shroud. This creates some serious problems that must be examined. The stay becomes the conductor and will be seriously damaged with current flow. The resistance, along with the connection to shroud and the plate in the water, is relatively high compared with copper. The plate itself is usually too small to effectively dissipate the strike energy, and lastly, corrosion issues must be addressed.

One innovative and portable device that incorporates all of the correct lightning protection elements is the Strikeshield system. This is connected to the mast or other down conducting item and it is connected to a 1/0 or 2/0 AWG shielded and tinned-copper cable. The cable is terminated with a specially designed dissipation electrode that is dropped into the water.

How to improve lightning grounding

A bridge or link should be installed between ground plate bolts, or at least two keel bolts, to distribute current evenly. A grounding system may have more than one grounding plate connected to the down conductor. Bridge out the two terminal bolts using a stainless steel link. This is to spread the contact area. In other cases, a large ground shoe can be used, or up to three smaller ground shoes can be configured in what is called a crow's foot principle. This radial system lowers the overall impedance to allow energy to diverge as each conductor and ground shoe takes a share of current. In a strike, the water permeating the sintered bronze ground shoe will literally boil, increasing local resistance, so any increase in surface areas will reduce this effect. The voltage gradients around the shoe will also be lower. The ground point must have sufficient area to adequately dissipate the strike energy. Links can also be drilled and used to bolt the ground cable connector, as many ground shoes have relatively small bolts designed for RF grounds only.

Making proper conductor joints

All connections shall be crimped; soldered joints shall not be used. Under no circumstances use soldered joints alone, as they will melt during a strike causing further havoc. On large cables, it is very difficult to ensure a good low resistance solder joint. After crimping, solder can be run in to enhance the joint, but this is not really necessary. Always crimp the connections and make sure that all bonded connections are clean and tight. All connections must be bolted to the ground point.

What about sidestrike protection?

All metallic items within 2 meters (6 ft) of the down conductor, termination and mast base or ground point shall be bonded to the lightning ground plate. Some recommendations call for rails, stanchions and all large metallic equipment, such as stainless water tanks, to be bonded to the lightning ground. It is only necessary to bond internal metallic equipment within six feet of the down conductor and bonding point. The bonding should be made at the point closest to the main conductor. Bonding conductors should be at least #8 AWG. The lightning bonding system should never be used as a negative return for any electrical circuit.

Figure 3-6 Sidestrike Effect

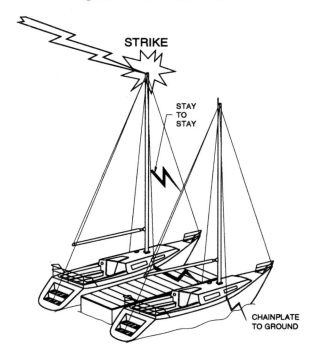

Interconnection of bonding systems

Ground plane potential equalization bonding between systems is designed to eliminate earth loops, differentials and reduce the level of potentially destructive transient currents that can flow when potential differences exist between the different unbonded grounding systems. In practice, there have been incidents where bonding of the cathodic protection system, power supply negatives and RF grounds have resulted in the vessel sinking as the thru-hull fittings have been blown out and all electrical and electronics systems destroyed. While many recommendations call for all these systems to be connected I prefer not to and do not support connection of a lightning protection system to anything connecting thru-hull fittings. The theory behind direct connection is to prevent induced rises in voltage within electrical circuit wiring and maintain them at a lower level. However, direct connection will allow a higher voltage to be impressed on circuits, and unlike induction, will allow actual current to flow.

Figure 3-7 Bonding and Grounding Arrangement

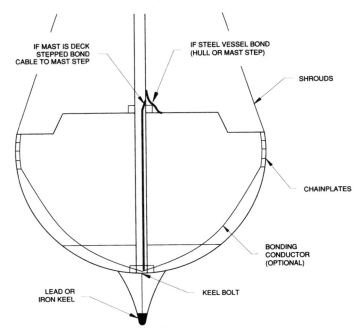

Surge, transient and static protection

Ideally, all electrical systems should have surge suppression devices fitted. It is common to have high levels of static build up on fiberglass decks in hot, dry, low humidity wind conditions. This causes significant static electricity shocks, so they require dissipation. The condition is common in the Mediterranean. In some cases, the process of arcing to ground as charges build up is a source of radio interference. Protection of sensitive electronics to transients is never easy. Ensure that metal cases are grounded in accordance with manufacturers' requirements. Most device cables are already made to maximize protection against induced interference.

Protecting the radio antennas

Aerials can draw a strike or have an induced current flow through the coaxial conductor to the radio. All antennas should have arresters fitted, although this is rarely done on boats. Antenna cables can be fitted with a two-way switch, one side to the radio, one to ground. You can buy remote and manual coax switches from companies such as NewMar. During a storm or if the vessel is left unattended, place the switch to ground position. Ideally an arrester or spark gap device can also be used. Coaxial cable surge protectors can also be used. Coaxial cable surge protectors via RF feeders are used even in shielded cables and triaxial cables, which will confine most current. Some induction can still occur due to magnetic and capacitive coupling.

Protecting DC power supplies

Power supplies should have double pole isolation on both positive and negative supplies. Additionally, surge suppression units can be installed which will clamp any over-voltage condition to a safe value, typically around 40 volts. All equipment can have what is called a transient protection device installed across the input power supply connections. These are generally metal oxide varistors (MOVs), available from electronics suppliers.

Protecting the AC power supplies

Efficient clamping and filtering at the power supply point requires surge diverters. The purpose is to limit residual voltages to a level within the immunity level range of the equipment. In 230VAC RMS systems damage can occur with just 700-volt peaks. Typical tolerances of battery chargers are under 800 volts. Some shunt devices can clamp the voltage at less than these voltages but they do not limit the fast wave front of the strike energy before clamping action starts. In a lightning strike, the rate of current rise can exceed 10kA/micro-seconds, and this can be greater in multiple strikes and re-strikes. Low pass filter technology, primary shunt diverters, will reduce the peak residual voltage and reduce rate of current and voltage rise reaching equipment. Surge reduction filters will provide multi-stage surge attenuation by clamping and then filtering the transients on power input circuits. These include metal oxide varistors (MOVs).

What is St. Elmo's Fire (brush discharge)?

This phenomenon is more common on steel vessels. When it occurs, it may precede a strike, although the effect does not occur all the time. The vessel in effect becomes a large ground mass. The discharge is characterized by ionized clouds and balls of white or green flashing light that polarize at vessel extremities. The discharge of negative ions reduces the potential intensity of a strike. Damage to electrical systems is usually induced into external wiring, as the steel hull acts as a large Faraday cage.

What is electromagnetic pulse (EMP)?

A vessel can have damaged equipment from a lightning strike within a few hundred yards. Insurance companies do not like to accept claims on damage unless you can show total damage to external masthead or other strike-damaged systems. A strike sends out a very large electromagnetic pulse, which is in effect a very strong magnetic field. This field induces into the wiring and systems a high-voltage spike, doing just as much damage as a direct hit. If you suspect damage from an induced electromagnetic pulse from a localized lightning strike, check with all vessels adjacent to yours, and get statements to support your contention. Generally, all the electronics will be out if this is the case because any external wiring acts like a large aerial.

Figure 3-8 Electromagnetic Pulse Effect

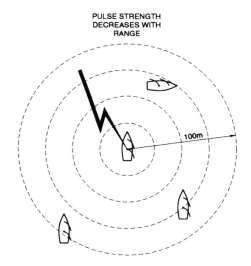

PULSE STRENGTH
DECREASES WITH
RANGE

100m

4.

INTERFERENCE

Troubleshooting RFI on radios and GPS

If you want to understand troubleshooting the problem of RFI on your electronics, then you have to understand the causes. The average boat has several RFI noise sources. These noises are often classified as Radio Frequency Interference (RFI) or Electromagnetic Interference (EMI). These are the insidious enemies of communications and electronics systems. They corrupt the GPS position fixes, make a mess of your communications, black out your fish finder screen and generally cause electronics performance degradation.

What is RFI?

Essentially RFI is noise that is superimposed as a disturbance or a voltage transient on the equipment. It can be impressed on the entire boat electrical power supply, or on the data and signal lines that carry your GPS or navigation data between each other. This noise is then processed along with all of the good data, and it will corrupt or degrade the processed information.

Where do the noises come from?

RFI noise occurs in a range of frequencies. In fact equipment may only be prone to problems within a specific frequency range. In many cases you will have multiple noise sources that overlay each other. This will result in a gradual degradation of the electronics components, and when the cumulative effects reach a critical point, the devices will fail.

What is a voltage transient?

The voltage transient is probably the most damaging and comes from many sources. Probably the best known effect is the corruption of your GPS and Loran data where the power is taken off an engine-starting battery. When a significant load is applied to the battery, such as starting the engine, a momentary voltage drop is created. What is often called a brown-out condition occurs, followed by a sharp voltage increase. This under-voltage disturbance can exceed 100 volts in some cases, damaging the power supplies, wiping memories or corrupting data. The same problem applies to dual battery systems where the house bank supplies power to items such as the electric toilets or windlass and other equipment with large current demand. The starting battery voltage can experience a 3- to 4-volt dip on a motor start-up. Transients are also caused by the variation or interruption of current in the equipment power conductor.

Figure 4-1 Transient Waveforms

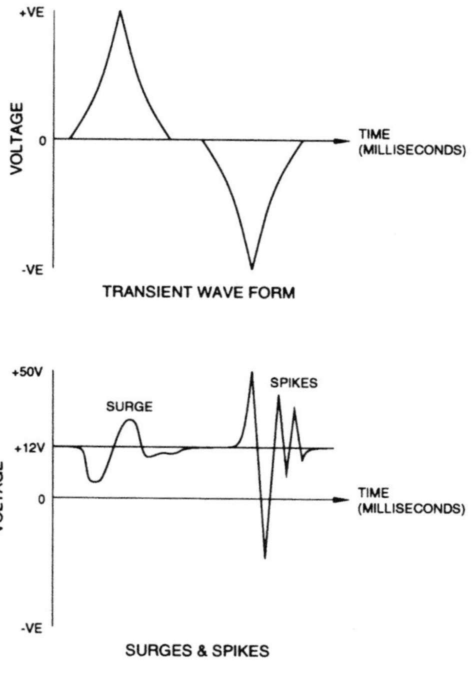

TRANSIENT WAVE FORM

SURGES & SPIKES

What is induced interference?

One common RFI noise source is called induced interference. Electrical fields radiate from all cables and equipment. This can be induced into other nearby cables or equipment. The most common cause of this problem are cables installed in parallel or within the same cable bundle, and this is called mutual coupling. Always make sure that the power supply cables and data cables are run separately and that the cables cross at 90 degrees. In particular run power cables to any sensitive equipment completely separate to the main power cables to reduce inductive and capacitive coupling to the data and signal conductors.

What is an arcing noise?

These are repetitive spikes caused by electric motor commutators and the sparking of brushes. The brushes on an alternator, particularly if they are dirty, can cause this sparking and noise. Charging systems where loose connections exist will create this problem. The most common cause is usually loose or poor engine return paths for alternators, when the negative path arcs across points of poor electrical contact. You should regularly check and tighten your negative terminals. Another cause is noise on ignition systems from distributors and spark plugs being impressed onto a DC system, often through radiation to adjacent cables. When troubleshooting, the first step is always to determine what is operating at the time.

About induced coupling interference

Electrical wires installed in parallel with other wires can suffer from what is termed inductive coupling interference. Buzzes and humming sounds are heard on the radio. This happens due to a transformer effect with a single turn primary and secondary coil, with the magnetic effects creating the induction. Low ground impedances and unbalanced circuits are the greatest source of problems with serial data, multi-cable control and co-axial cables being the most susceptible to noise. Again it is best to keep all signal cables installed separately so you don't have parallel runs with the main power wiring. The first step in troubleshooting RFI is to determine what equipment is operating at the time, because this will directly affect the cables involved and will aid in fault finding.

What is ripple noise?

Ripple is created in rectifier bridges (such as the diode or SCR bridge). These are found in charging alternators, battery chargers, fluorescent lights and AC inverters. It usually is a high-pitched whine sound on radios. Most good quality equipment will have suppressed electronics. Ripple badly degrades audio quality on radios. As before, determine which lights are operating, whether a charger is on, and whether the engine is running. It is often a sign that an alternator diode has blown.

About surge (electromagnetic pulse)

This interference is caused by local lightning activity. The pulses are generally induced into electrical wiring and radios or other aerials.

What is a spike?

Turn-on spikes result from the initial charging of input filters on power supplies. Turn-off spikes happen when reactive loads are switched, and the magnetic fields collapse on inductive loads, such as transformers, relay or contactor coils, solenoid coils, pump motors, etc. MOV suppressors are often put across the coils.

About static charges

Static charges have several sources. External charge interference usually appears due to static build-up in sailboat rigging. On reaching a certain voltage level, the static discharges to the ground, which causes the interference on radios. Another common source is when dry offshore winds occur, and a high net static charge builds up on fiberglass (GRP) decks. This problem is more prevalent on larger fiberglass vessels such as catamarans with relatively large deck surface areas. A lightning protection system can ground out these static charges. The engine and propeller shaft can also accumulate charges when rotating. Interference is caused when the accumulated charges ground out. These charges arise because of static build-up, both induced and due to the interaction of moving parts in the engine. The static charge will discharge to ground when it reaches a high voltage level and will also cause RFI interference.

About solar activity

This source of RFI is from activity and changes within the iono-sphere, and solar or sun spot activity. The main result is signal losses or major data corruption. It is best to verify that there is no current major solar activity. This often happens around sunset.

How do you start troubleshooting RFI?

Now that you know the source of all this RFI you can start trou-bleshooting RFI. By systematically switching off each piece of equipment, you will be able to locate the source of the trouble-some noise. When the noise stops the cause is generally located. While it is a simple process of elimination, it isn't always so easy. Most cases will involve the identification of two or more noise sources that are overlaid to create a cumulative noise effect. Some RFI noise will be intermittent, and this includes static discharges and lightning pulses, which will not be easy to identify.

What tools do you need?

The best RFI sniffing tool is a cheap battery-powered AM radio. This is a great little tool for tracking down those radiated sources on the boat. When the radio is close to the cables or equipment, it will detect the noise. Some noise is related to the time of day. Interference from solar activity and ionosphere factors on radios is one source that must always be factored in. These sources will affect your GPS, SSB and HAM radios and satellite communica-tions all simultaneously, leading to a greater problem. This usu-ally occurs around dusk. Wait until later and try your radios again, and you may already have the answer.

Troubleshooting GPS noise

The first step in troubleshooting the noise on the GPS or radios is to disconnect the antenna. If the noise continues, it is probably caused by the electrical system. If the RFI tends to increase when the GPS or radios aerials are reconnected, the cause may be atmospheric or from some other emission source that is being picked up through the antenna feed cables. It is important to remember that RFI may be coming from more than one source or path, so investigate all possibilities.

Why is there a ticking sound on the radio?

If the noise on your radio shows up as a ticking noise that seems to vary with the speed of the engine, you are probably picking up ignition noise, or it is coming from the alternator. In practice, this would affect the power wire to the equipment. The most common sources for this noise are the distributor, ignition coil, spark plug wires and the spark plugs. If the ignition noise is identified, relocate the power wire as far as possible from any of these sources. If things don't improve, then check all of these components. It is prudent to verify that the spark plug wires and the spark plugs are RFI shielded.

Which noise suppression method is best?

There are several methods available to reduce or eliminate RFI interference. The first is the use of shielded cables along with proper grounding. Suppressors such as a filter or capacitor connected close to the noise-causing equipment are common. This effectively short-circuits the noise in the protected frequency range. Suppression filters can be of several types and suppressor capacitors are often required on alternators.

Figure 4-2 Noise Filtering and Stabilization

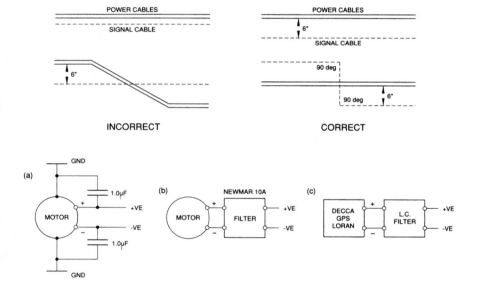

About grounding

If you want to obtain optimum electronics performance, the grounding must be installed properly. The majority of RFI problems, including the noises, hums, buzzes, interference or cross talk on your radios, often result from poor grounding practices. A difference in voltage between the two different ground points will cause current flow and therefore problems. The currents that flow through the different grounds are called ground loops. The ground in any GPS and radio electronics system is the reference voltage point for all signals. It is nominally equal to 0 volt. To prevent ground loops from arising, all of the signal grounds should be connected to one single common ground point.

Cable shields are designed to protect against interference from unknown or unspecified sources. The effectiveness of cable shields is measured in terms of transfer impedance. This is a measure of effectiveness in capturing the interference field and preventing it from reaching the conductor pairs inside. Signal and data cables also have shields that are made from foil/polymer laminate tapes or with layers of copper braiding. These may also have a drain wire installed to facilitate the termination of the screen to ground. In general, most equipment manufacturers will nominate the termination of shields to ground. You should never ground the cable screen at both ends, but only ground at one end, usually nominated as the equipment end. Very often cable shields are not connected at all. Always check and connect them, as it may be a source of your elusive RFI.

Figure 4-3 Grounding and Screening

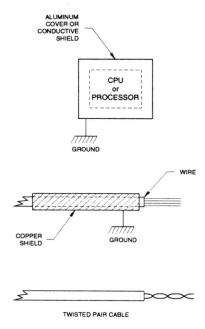

ALUMINUM
COVER OR
CONDUCTIVE
SHIELD

CPU
or
PROCESSOR

GROUND

WIRE

COPPER
SHIELD

GROUND

TWISTED PAIR CABLE

What causes trolling motor interference?

Interference often occurs on fishfinders and GPS. This is caused by some trolling motor pulse width modulation (PWM) speed control systems. Some LCD displays may go to a solid black, or just blank out. Flasher-type sounders may stop flashing. It is more common on trolling-motor-mounted transducers. The interference really depends on the make and type of sounder, where it is located, where the transducer is installed, and how the wiring is installed. The worst cases appear to be when fishfinders are set in manual mode with high gain or sensitivity settings, and low speed motor operation. The most common error is the fastening of the transducer cable to the power cable or the foot pedal assembly cable.

How to track down the noise sources

It is best to do a noise check on all boats. Operate all equipment, bilge pumps, trolling motors, bait livewell aerator pumps, power tilt and trim control, tachometers, fishfinder (with sensitivity set to 75%). If noise or interference is observed, systematically switch each item off until the noise disappears. Sometimes two or more pieces of equipment may have relatively low noise levels but be cumulative. If the trolling motor is found to be the cause, place the motor in the high by-pass mode. This will usually stop the noise and prove that it is the PWM control. Noise can also be caused by bad grounds; bad wiring is not usually the cause.

How to stop trolling motor interference

If the cause of noise is found to be the trolling motor, there are several remedies to consider. The first is the connection of the trolling motor. The supply wiring should go directly to the battery, and in some cases, if electronics are connected, they may have to be connected to another battery. The second solution is the routing of the supply cables. The motor cables should be installed as far as possible from other wiring, preferably on the opposite side of the boat. The transducer wiring should not be too close to the trolling motor wiring. In severe cases, the transducer may have to be moved to a new location. If the boat is fiberglass, the internal transducer relocation is relatively easy. In some cases the fishfinder power supply may have to be connected directly to the outboard cranking battery. Depending on the location of the transducer, the cables should be installed and strapped to the outside of the trolling motor. The transducer cable should not be fastened in the control loom from the footswitch or power supply. Motorguide has a RF choke available. The sonar cable is wrapped 5 turns around half of the clamshell RF choke. This should be as close as possible to the sonar and it filters out noise to the sonar. On many boats, accessories and forward-mounted sounders are powered off the trolling motor batteries. The grounds and negatives must all be held at the same level to reduce noise. Pinpoint has developed a range of interference-free 20° puck transducers. The patent-pending design shields the transducer from electrical noise generated within PWM speed controls.

Grounding trolling motors

The motor must be grounded to the boat's common ground. If ungrounded, interference levels may be higher and also may increase corrosion. The ground of the small boat is to the negative side of the battery. The ground jumper is connected from the negative to the casing inside the pedal assembly on the Motorguide Tour Edition. In the 36-volt units an additional cable is installed back to the battery negative. In hand-operated models, an additional cable is fastened to the upper shaft with a hose clamp and taken back to the battery negative. It is best to solder bare cable for about 1 inch, and fold it once before inserting it under the clamp. Cover with self-amalgamating tape to protect it from weather.

Fishfinder interference.

If your fishfinder has interference, a possible source is the trolling motor. Noise can also come from other electrical equipment and the outboard engine. This can show up as display blank outs, random targets or stray pixels, lines on the display, or no key functions. In some cases, two fishfinders may be running at the same time. Two boats in close proximity may cause mutual interference if they are using similar acoustic frequencies. If you are running two fishfinders, they need to have frequencies at least 20kHz apart. If the interference is present with all systems off, the fishfinder automatic noise rejection facility may be malfunctioning. Zercom has overcome the interference from other fishfinders by having dual frequency sounders between the front and rear. Vexilar has what is called the S-Cable that attenuates the power output by 70%. This is used in shallow or weed areas. The sensitivity usually has to be decreased, as the power output is too high for the shallow depths. This allows two stages of gain reduction, one on power output and one for the unit. In some cases the sounder will have to be connected to a different battery to that being charged, in systems using series connections for 24- or 36-volts, connect to the same battery with other circuits connected. Sometimes interference will start as the spark plugs degrade. The majority of outboard engines have resistor-type spark plugs fitted. On some boats, the tachometer is the cause of the interference. It should be disconnected at the engine to verify, and may require rerouting cables. The charging system is also a possible cause. When the sounder has a filter, make sure this is selected to <ON>.

Acknowledgements

Thanks and appreciation go to the following companies for their assistance. Readers are encouraged to contact them for equipment advice and supply. Quality equipment is part of reliability

M G Duff	www.mgduff.co.uk
Latham Marine	www.zincsmart.com
Strikeshield	www.strikeshield.com
Forespar	www.forespar.com
Western Solid State	www.wss-ltd.com
Lowrance	www.lowrance.com

Log on to the author's website
www.fishingandboats.com

Index